Praise for Harvey's 7 *New York Times* Bestselling Books

"Harvey Mackay may be the most talented man I have met."

—Lou Holtz

"If anyone can 'write the book' on sales success, it's Harvey Mackay. He is a proven leader in sales. My advice: Follow the leader to a stellar sales career!"

—John C. Maxwell

"Harvey Mackay is a champ at sales—and he doesn't pull any punches with his heavyweight advice."

—Muhammad Ali

"In today's world the only thing that you have going for you is YOU. But are you the best YOU, you can be? Now a book that can guide you to be more and have more."

—Suze Orman

"Don't share this book with your competition; share it with your people. I'm going to do just that. Will it make a difference? Your competitors won't like the answer."

—Ken Blanchard

"There are three kinds of business experts. There's an expert, there's a world-class expert, and there's Harvey Mackay—THE world-class expert."

—Jeffrey Gitomer

"A mother lode of timely, hard-earned, bite-size, streetsmart golden nuggets … invaluable for job seekers, employed or unemployed."

—Stephen Covey

"He is fast, smart, funny … and frighteningly right."

—Gloria Steinem

"Enjoy Harvey's cookbook for success … It gives the reader the best of his wisdom … truly the best kind of chicken soup for anyone and everyone in business and in life."

—Mark Victor Hansen and Jack Canfield

"Harvey's business acumen shows through on every page … There's so much warmth, wisdom, and wittiness in this book that it would be well for everyone to read every page."

—Billy Graham

"Harvey Mackay is the only person I'll listen to while standing in shark-infested waters … real stories from the real world with real solutions."

—Larry King

"Harvey Mackay is one of the greatest writers of our time."

—Norman Vincent Peale

Harvey Mackay's

ABCs
OF
SUCCESS

**MADE FOR
SUCCESS**

Made for Success Publishing
P.O. Box 1775 Issaquah, WA 98027
www.MadeForSuccessPublishing.com

Distributed by Made for Success Publishing

First Printing

Library of Congress Cataloging-in-Publication data

MacKay, Harvey
  Harvey Mackay's ABCs of Success

       p. cm.

LCCN: 2022905607
ISBN: 978-1-64146-582-3 (*Paperback*)
ISBN: 978-1-64146-583-0 (*eBook*)

            Printed in the United States of America

                For further information
          contact Made for Success Publishing
     +14255266480 or email service@madeforsuccess.net

Contents

Introduction

Many years ago, I was listening as one of my grand-children practiced his ABCs. He had a little picture book that helped him remember what the letters stood for, and he studied it intently, determined to be the first in his class to know all the letters and words. With his determination, I knew he would master the alphabet in no time at all.

As he worked, I started thinking about what those letters mean to me after a lifetime in sales and years of helping young hopefuls get started in their careers.

What a marvelous invention the alphabet is! My career has spanned six decades, and yet, I find an exercise I learned before kindergarten to be among the most helpful tools at my disposal.

For a writer and speaker, the uses are quite obvious. I particularly appreciate the logical organization method it provides. And because I need to organize my thoughts, topics and concepts in every facet of my presentations, books and columns, the alphabet makes a very convenient starting point.

The same is true for organizing my business. Starting at point A makes perfect sense, laying out a clear path so that I can assess progress toward my goal.

I didn't draw pictures, but these are the words my alphabet book would include.

***Mackay's Moral:**
You don't need a big close, as many
sales reps believe. You risk losing
your customer when you save
all the good stuff for the end.
Keep the customer actively involved
throughout your presentation,
and watch your results improve.*

THE ABCs of
SELLING

The first list I developed, the ABCs of Selling, was so well received that I decided to write another list, and then another and another and another. The topics I chose are central to my business dealings, my volunteer activities, and my life in general. I want readers to understand that the title words of these chapters are related to every kind of career.

And even though the explanations are brief, they get to the heart of the matter. A few letters of the alphabet describe some of the deeper meanings, and, I hope, give the reader something to consider as they put these different concepts into practice.

A is for availability for your customers,

so they can reach you with questions, concerns or reorders.

If I can't reach you immediately, I want to know that you'll get back to me within minutes or hours, not days. If you're slow to answer the call, your phone will stop ringing.

B is for believe in your product,

or find something else to sell. It's also important to believe in yourself.

C is for customers aren't always right,

but if you want to keep them as your customers, find a way to make them right.

D is for deliver more than you promise.

Never make a promise you can't keep.

E is for education is for life – never stop learning.

Education is an investment, never an expense.

F is for follow up and follow through.

Never leave a customer hanging. I like to say that the sale begins when the customer says yes – every sales person knows that following through after the order is written is what earns customer loyalty.

G is for goals,

which give you a reason to go to work every day. When you reach your goals, set higher ones!

H is for humanize your selling strategy

by learning everything you can about your customers.

To be successful in life – and especially in sales – you must have a deep-down burning desire to help people. Studies show that you can't talk business all the time. Your customers are people first!

I is the least important letter in selling.

Unity consistently produces greater results than individual endeavors. Teamwork divides the effort and multiplies the effect.

J is for join trade organizations and community groups

that will help you both professionally and personally, such as Toastmasters, chamber of commerce, or Junior Achievement.

K is for know your competitors

and their products as well as you know your own.

Sam Walton, creator of Walmart, the world's largest retail chain, spent more time in Kmart than his own stores. Information is power.

L is for listen to your customers,

or they'll start talking to someone else.

We learn more by listening than talking. Remember, most people won't listen to what you're saying unless they already feel that you have listened to them. Being a good listener can make or break a career.

M is for maybe, the worst answer a customer can give.

No is better than maybe. Find out what you can do to turn it into a yes.

N is for networking,

which is among the most important skills a salesperson can develop. Someone you know knows someone you need to know.

O is for opportunities are everywhere.

Keep your antennae up.

P is for price,

which is not the only reason customers buy your product, but it's a good reason.

Q is for quality,

which can never be sacrificed if you want to keep your customers satisfied.

R is for relationships are precious.

They take time to develop and are worth every minute you invest in them. If you want one year of prosperity, you grow grain. If you want 10 years of prosperity, you grow trees. But if you want 100 years of prosperity, you grow relationships.

S is for service is spelled "serve us"

in companies that want to stay in business for a long time.

Most customers who complain don't really want their money back. They just want products or services that work the way they're supposed to. They want someone who will listen to them and fix any problem that arises.

T is for trust, the most important word in business.

Trust is central to doing business with anyone. Trust is telling the truth, even when it is difficult, and being truthful and trustworthy in your dealings with customers and staff. It takes years to build up trust, but only seconds to destroy it. Without trust, you have another word that begins with T: trouble.

U is for unlimited potential

is possible whether you sell computers or candy.

You are the only one who can limit your potential.

V is for volunteer.

It's always good to give back.

You'll probably find that you get more than you give, and there is no shortage of organizations that need your help. People who do volunteer work and help others on a regular basis have a healthier outlook on life. They are inclined to be go-getters and consistently report being happier and more contented.

W is for winning doesn't necessarily mean beating everyone else.

A win-win situation is the best of both worlds. Legendary professional football coach Vince Lombardi said: "Winning is not a sometime thing; it's an all time thing. You don't win once in a while, you don't do things right once in a while, you do them right all the time. Winning is habit. Unfortunately, so is losing."

X is for x-ray and CAT scan your customers

so that you know everything about them – so you can serve them better.

We want to know through routine conversation what turns that customer on – hobbies, interests, concerns.

Y is for you,

a word your customers need to hear often, as in "What can I do for you?"

Z is for zeal,

a critical element in your presentations, service and life in general.

Let your enthusiasm shine through!

Some things never change – including the importance of knowing how to treat your customers and
what really matters in your relationships. And as
you can see, most of these items cover far more
than just sales.

Someday, I think my grandchildren will still be
able to use my little alphabet book. Nothing would
make me prouder.

Mackay's Moral:
Now you know my ABCs –
sales skills from A to Z.

THE ABCs of
NEGOTIATING

As a kid, I practiced the art of negotiating daily with my parents and teachers. I continued to hone my skills as I grew, eventually buying a small struggling envelope company. Over decades as a business owner and salesman, I've probably spent as much time in negotiations as any other part of my job.

More deals result from whom you know than what you know. And, it's not just who you know but how you get to know them. Always aim to build contacts on an even footing.

You also have to have a feel for the deal. There is no more certain recipe for disaster than a decision based on emotion. Make decisions with your heart, and you'll end up with heart disease.

As for pricing, it's not how much something is worth; it's how much people think it's worth. There is no such thing as a final offer.

These valuable lessons have become my ABCs of negotiating.

A is for authority.

Always, before you start any negotiation, look beyond the title and make sure that the person you're dealing with is in a position of authority to sign off on the agreement. If not, don't deal until you can sit down with someone who is.

B is for beware the naked man who offers you his shirt.

If the customer can't or won't pay what the deal is worth, you don't need the sale. Never go broke to get a deal.

C is for contracts.

The most important term in any contract isn't in the contract. It's dealing with people who are honest. Whenever someone says, "Forget the contract, our word is good enough," maybe yours is, but his or hers usually isn't. Rotten wood cannot be carved.

D is for dream.

A dream is always a bargain no matter what you pay for it.

E is for experience.

When a person with money meets a person with experience, the person with the experience winds up with the money, and the person with the money winds up with the experience.

F is for facts.

Gather all the facts you can on both sides of the negotiation. Remember, knowledge does not become power until it is used.

G is for guts.

It takes plenty of guts to hold firm on your position, and just as many to know when to make concessions.

H is for honesty.

Not only is it the best policy, it is the only policy. Your reputation for honest dealings will keep doors open that get slammed in others' faces.

I is for information.

In the long run, instincts are no match for information. The most powerful weapon you can possess in any negotiation is superior information.

J is for jungle.

The law of the jungle is "survival of the fittest." Be ready to defend your position or walk away if your position is threatened.

K is for know about no.

If you can't say yes, it's no. Period. Don't sugarcoat it. Don't talk yourself into yes just to seem like a nice guy. No one ever went broke because he or she ever said no too much.

L is for leaks.

The walls have ears. Don't discuss any business where it can be overheard by others. Almost as many deals have gone down in elevators as elevators have gone down.

M is for market.

You cannot negotiate anything unless you absolutely know the market.

N is for never say no for the other person.

Make them turn down the deal, not you. Don't jump to conclusions that they won't or can't lower the price, improve the terms, or sweeten the deal in countless ways.

O is for options.

Keep your options open, because the first negotiation isn't usually the only negotiation.

P is for positioning.

They can always tell when you need the sale more than they need the deal.

Q is for questions.

Question every angle, motive, and outcome. Not out loud necessarily, but so that you are satisfied that you understand the opposition's strategy and can respond.

R is for reality check.

In any negotiation, the given reason is seldom the real reason. When someone says no based on price, money is almost never the real reason.

S is for smile – and say no, no, no until your tongue bleeds.

If the deal isn't right for you, stay calm, stay pleasant and just say no.

T is for timing.

People go around all their lives saying, "What should I buy? What should I sell?" Wrong questions! "When should I buy? When should I sell?" Timing is everything.

U is for ultimatum.

Never give an ultimatum unless you mean it.

V is for variables.

Anticipate what variables you are willing to change, the objections that will be tossed back at you, and your response to those.

W is for win-win.

A negotiation doesn't have to have a winner and a loser. Everyone should come out winning something. A deal can always be made when the parties see it to their own benefit.

X is for eXit strategy.

Decide in advance when you will withdraw from negotiating, when you can no longer achieve what you need or when the other side cannot be trusted to negotiate fairly.

Y is for yield.

What will this deal yield for you? What will you have to yield to make it work?

Z is for zero

in on what you want, what you need, and what you are willing to concede.

Mackay's Moral:
Agreements prevent disagreements.

THE ABCs of
CUSTOMER
SERVICE

Whatever business you are in – manufacturing, retail, health care, travel, high tech – you must realize that first and foremost, you are in the service business.

We all know how we like to be treated when we conduct a transaction. We also know how we do not like to be treated. There is no excuse not to render exceptional customer service.

But it has always amazed me that some organizations expect their customers to put up with disappointing service. It's so much easier in the long run to expend a little more effort into putting your best foot forward.

So based on personal experience and extensive research, I offer my ABCs for customer service.

A is for anticipate.

Know what your customers need, what problems may arise, and how you can best serve them. Don't just meet their needs, anticipate them. Don't wait for them to tell you there's a problem. Go out and ask them.

B is for business.

Customer service is your business, no matter what you make or what service you provide. Keep repeating that mantra. Improve your service to improve your business.

C is for commitments.

You vouch for planned delivery dates, not random drop-off times. Businesses live on commitments, which lead to steady repeat sales. It's not about what you can do; it's about what you will do.

D is for details.

No detail is too small to a customer who has come to expect perfection from you. Little things mean a lot … not true. Little things mean everything.

E is for empowerment.

Every single person on your payroll must be empowered to make decisions on the spot that accommodate the customer first. The most important person in every single company is the frontline employee who works directly with customers.

F is for fix the problem fast and fix it well.

When, despite your best efforts, something goes wrong, find out the reason and correct it immediately. It may cost you big time, but it will pay off in the future.

G is for give customers what they want.

Many don't really want their money back. They just want products or services that work the way they're supposed to. Disappoint customers and they'll disappear.

H is for hiring the right people

to create and maintain a service culture.

Recognize the skills and attitude you want, and make sure your staff supports that vision. You cannot be good at customer service unless you understand one four-letter word in the dictionary … HIRE.

I is for the Internet.

Customer service has taken on a whole new meaning with the rise of social media and websites like Angi and Yelp. Google your company and see what you find. Refer to letter F if you don't like what you see. Bad customer service reviews can span the globe instantly. Good reviews can too.

J is for journey.

Great service is not a one-time event, it's an ongoing trek over weeks or years that comes with plenty of twists and turns to navigate. Set your standards high, and don't accept anything less from yourself or your employees.

K is for keep your word.

Honesty and trust go hand in hand. Your word is your reputation, and your reputation is your future. Your reputation is worth more than all the machinery and inventory you own. Once customer confidence is lost, getting it back is harder than starting out from scratch.

L is for long-term customer loyalty.

It is not a hit and miss thing. You court it. You earn it. You cultivate it. You retain it.

M is for management,

which needs to give employees the authority to help people before there is a problem, or be prepared to step in and handle the matter themselves. Look at all policies, procedures and systems that you have in place that make life miserable for customers and correct them.

N is for no customer service equals no customers.

I've yet to see a business that can survive without customers.

O is for the other guys.

What are they doing that you should be doing better? Make it a practice to study competitors to see what they have to offer.

P is for performance.

If there was an award for best performance in a customer-service setting, you should be a shoo-in. Be aware of every opportunity to outperform your competition. Make your customers number one, and they'll make you number one.

Q is for quick-witted.

Be prepared to make adjustments to satisfy your customers. Find a way to give them what they need and want as quickly as possible.

R is for rebound,

which is what you need to do to regain a customer's business.

First, admit your mistake. Next, offer a solution to demonstrate your sincere desire to make things right. Third, express your intention to never make the same mistake again. And finally, learn from the experience to train your staff.

S is for satisfaction.

Your goal is satisfied customers, even when you can't give them exactly what they want. Great service is, in my estimation, probably more important than either price or quality. But without a combination of the three, your customers will be shopping around. Give them the total package.

T is for take care of your customers or someone else will.

If you don't serve your customer, they'll serve notice. Taking care of customers is taking care of business.

U is for under-promise and over-deliver.

There has never been a sounder approach to customer service and sales. There is no such thing as too good where customer service is involved.

V is for value.

Customers need to value your product, your service and your relationship. Give them every reason to value you. And make sure they know you value them.

W is for wow,

as in constantly finding ways to wow your customers.

Make every encounter as special as you can, because your customers will remember how you made them feel.

X is for eXpress lane.

There is no traffic jam in going the extra mile – and great customer service is your path to success.

Y is for years.

Your goal is to have a customer for life. I firmly believe that respect is earned, honesty is appreciated, and loyalty is returned.

Z is for zealous.

If you want to set up and run a business with longevity in the form of long-term and repeating customers, you have to service those clients with zealous enthusiasm.

__Mackay's Moral:__
*Customer Service is not just
another department;
it's everyone's job.*

THE ABCs of
NETWORKING

If I had to name the single characteristic shared by all the truly successful people I've met over a lifetime, I'd say it is the ability to create and nurture a network of contacts. I could lose all my money and all my factories, but leave me my contacts and I'll be back as strong as ever in three to five years. Networking is that important.

The alphabet is a great place to start as you build your network – organize your contacts from A to Z. Then organize your networking skills. Now it's time for the ABCs of networking.

A is for antennae,

which should be up every waking moment.

Never pass up an opportunity to meet new people.

B is for birthdays.

It's always advantageous to know the birthdays of your contacts. You wouldn't believe how much business our sales reps write up when they call on their customers' birthdays.

C is for contact management system.

Have your data organized so that you can cross reference entries and find the information you need quickly. When you work on your network, your network works for you.

D is for dig your well before you're thirsty.

People aren't strangers if you've already met them. The trick is to meet them *before* you need their help.

E is for exchange and expand.

When two people exchange dollar bills, each still has only one dollar. But when two people exchange networks, they each have access to two networks.

F is for Facebook and all other social media.

These sites open unlimited possibilities for networking. Use them wisely. The more you exercise your networking muscles, the stronger they get – the easier networking becomes.

G is for gatekeeper.

There usually is a trusted assistant trained to block or grant your access. Don't waste their time, and make sure you acknowledge their significant role in reaching the boss. Getting through the fence to the top dog is easy, if you know the gatekeeper.

H is for hearing.

Make note of news you hear affecting someone in your network so you can reference it at the appropriate time. Put your memory where your mouth is. If you want to impress people with how much you care, show them how much you remember.

I is for intelligence.

You can't (and shouldn't) talk about business all the time. Learn everything you can about your contacts' families, pets, hobbies, and interests.

J is for job security,

which you will always have if you develop a good network.

As the world changes, one thing will remain constant: the relationships you develop over a lifetime.

K is for keeping in touch.

If your network is going to work, you have to stay plugged in and keep the wires humming. I have never once heard a successful person say he or she regretted putting time and energy into their network.

L is for lessons.

The first real networking school I signed up for after I graduated from college was Toastmasters. Dale Carnegie schools are designed to achieve similar goals.

M is for multiply.

Don't just add to your number of contacts, multiply their worth. Surveys show that every person knows approximately 200 people, which means that every person has potentially 40,000 contacts.

N is for nurturing your network.

What can you do to help them?

Two things people never forget: Those who were caring to them when they were at a low point, and those who weren't.

O is for outgoing.

Be the first to introduce yourself, lend a hand, or send congratulations for a job well done. It does matter *how* they remember you, but it's more important that they *do* remember you.

P is for people.

You have to love people to be a good networker. Dale Carnegie probably summed it up best: "You can make more friends in two months by becoming really interested in other people than you can in two years by trying to get other people interested in you."

Q is for quilt.

Your network should be a crazy quilt of contacts that help form the fabric of your life.

R is for reciprocity.

You give; you get. You no give; you no get. If you only do business with people you know and like, you won't be in business very long.

S is for six degrees of separation,

the thought that there is a chain of no more than six people that link every person. Someone you know knows someone who knows someone you want to know.

T is for telephone.

Landline, cell, internet – this is a critical tool for staying in touch with your network.

U is for urgency.

Don't be slow to answer the call, even if you never expect to have your effort repaid.

V is for visibility.

You've got to get involved in organizations and groups to get connected, but don't confuse visibility with credibility. You have to give in order to get.

W is not only for whom you know,

but also for who knows you.

X is for the eXtra mile.

Your network contacts will go the extra mile for you, and you must be willing to do the same for them.

Y is for yearly check-in.

Find a way, even if it's just a holiday card, to stay in touch.

Z is for zip code.

Do you have plenty represented in your network?

Mackay's Moral:
You don't have to know everything
as long as you know the people
who do.

THE ABCs of
ENTREPRENEURSHIP

I was recently asked by master marketer Jay Abraham to appear on his radio program, "The Ultimate Entrepreneur" along with several others including Stephen Covey and Mark Cuban. In that company, I knew I had my work cut out for me!

Start with the basics: What better way than to create the ABCs of entrepreneurship? As I have developed my version of the ABCs of a variety of business practices, I've discovered how much they help me focus on new ways of looking at potential ventures.

A is for ability.

Entrepreneurs excel at identifying problems and solving them fast. They anticipate obstacles and opportunities. You have to believe in your ability and capitalize on your strengths. There is always room at the table for those who are able.

B is for business plan.

A successful entrepreneur must make one before doing anything else. People don't plan to fail; they fail to plan. And remember, a plan isn't a plan until you have a backup plan.

C is for cash,

because all entrepreneurs need money.

Use it wisely, even when you are rolling in it. There is no substitute for crisp, crunchy, crackly, cold, hard cash.

D is for delegate.

You know what you do well and what you do poorly. Decide what to outsource and delegate these tasks to others. When you delegate you elevate.

E is for ethics.

If you have integrity, nothing else matters. If you don't have integrity, nothing else matters. If truth stands in your way, you're headed in the wrong direction. Always act like your mother is watching.

F is for failure.

Few entrepreneurs make it the first time they try. If you can survive it to fight again, you haven't failed. Failure is merely the opportunity to start over again, wiser than before.

G is for giving

because givers are the biggest gainers.

If you truly believe in what you are doing, give it all you've got. Greatness lies in helping somebody, not in trying to be somebody.

H is for humor,

as in don't take things too seriously.

You are going to experience tough times and humor helps pull you through. Every survival kit should include a sense of humor. He or she who laughs, lasts!

I is for interpersonal relationships.

Those with good people skills are able to adjust and survive as their business grows. Good relationships will help you deal with life's minor annoyances and your most challenging problems.

J is for journal,

as in writing down your thoughts and ideas, as well as picking the brains of experts.Don't forget to review your journal periodically for things you forgot, missed, or overlooked.

K is for knowledgeable.

Successful entrepreneurs are constantly updating themselves regarding their product and industry. Knowledge does not become power until it is used.

L is for looking forward.

A successful entrepreneur looks ahead, around corners, and as far into the future as possible.

M is for mentor.

Find a "tiger," preferably someone who's been around the block. Retired professionals are a marvelous resource for this kind of advice. And remember, mentors change over a lifetime. Mentoring presents a tremendous win-win opportunity that few business relationships offer. And who doesn't want to be a winner?

N is for never give up.

Amend your plans if needed, but keep your eye on the prize. The hardest sale you'll ever make is to yourself. But once you're convinced you can do it, you can.

O is for offerings.

Whether you see a need that is unfulfilled, or a product that could be improved, or a problem screaming for a solution, you are seeing an opportunity to offer something new and different.

P is for passion.

When you have passion, you speak with conviction, act with authority, and present with zeal. There is no substitute for passion. If you don't have a deep-down, intense, burning desire for what you are doing, there's no way you'll be able to work the long, hard hours it takes to become successful.

Q is for quantify.

Your goals must be measurable, so it's necessary to have a standard to hold them to. You can't keep track of your progress if you don't know where you want to go.

R is for risk.

Entrepreneurs must be willing to take risks. Sometimes you have to triple your failure rate to triple your success.

S is for self-survey.

Do you really want to do this or are you just trying to escape your own problems? If you're going to be an entrepreneur, you have to believe in yourself more than you believe in anything else in the world.

T is for target audience.

If your concept is going to succeed, you have to identify a realistic target audience, big enough to be profitable yet small enough for you to service it thoroughly.

U is for unflappable.

Beyond the "don't sweat the small stuff" mentality, you need to keep a level head and an open mind.

V is for veracity.

The truth, the whole truth, and nothing but the truth is what your employees and customers deserve from you. Anything less will earn you a bad reputation.

W is for work hard.

And then work harder. And keep working as hard as you can until you get the results you are looking for. And then keep working hard.

X is for eXercise regularly.

If you don't take care of yourself, you can't be at your best.

Y is for yearning.

You must have a deep yearning to work so hard to get your idea off the ground.

Z is for zookeeper.

When you're running the place, it's up to you to keep the dangerous things in their cages while bringing the visitors through the gates.

Mackay's Moral:
Being an entrepreneur is a lot like
the ABCs — start at the beginning
and follow your plan through
to the end.

THE ABCs of
MANAGEMENT

As I began this list of management ABCs, I was determined not to confuse management with leadership. There are leaders at all levels, whether we identify them with a special title or simply recognize their ability to direct their colleagues. Managers, on the other hand, have responsibilities to the organization to achieve results, often by working with the leaders.

Here are my thoughts on what managers need to know.

A is for advice.

Good advice doesn't get old. Good advice is never cheap, and cheap advice is never good.

B is for bringing out the best

in others to get them to believe in what you believe in: your employees.

C is for caring is contagious.

Help spread it around. People don't care how much you know about them once they realize how much you care about them.

D is for diverse.

A good team is a collection of people with diverse ideas who respect each other and are committed to each other's successes.

E is for excellence.

Managers should demand nothing less than excellence because they have set an example of demanding excellence from themselves.

F is for first.

Running your own business is no endeavor for anyone who feels anything other than the urge to be the first person in the door in the morning and the one they have to drag out at night.

G is for good.

The trick isn't to get good at everything in your business. The trick is getting to know what you are good at and figuring out how to get better.

H is for hero.

As much as you would like to be a hero, look to the heroes in your company and acknowledge and encourage their contributions. I've always admired people who pulled others up the ladder.

I is for impression.

What's the easiest way to check the first impression you're making? Have someone call your company to check up on how the call is handled. Find out what your customers already know about your business.

J is for judging.

We consciously or unconsciously judge a lot of companies by the attitudes of their average workers – the store clerk, driver, receptionist, and so on. Don't underestimate their impact.

K is for kindness.

Treat yourself and others with respect. Plant seeds of kindness by doing something kind every day. Every form of kindness you show doesn't bounce, it reproduces itself. If you are too busy to be kind, you are too busy.

L is for listen.

You can't learn anything if you are doing all the talking. Listen to your staff because they often have great solutions and ideas for improvement. Two ears, one mouth: nature's way of telling you to listen more than you talk.

M is for money.

Managing money is as important as managing people. If you don't manage your resources well, you'll have to manage the mess you've made.

N is for nice,

as in nice guys can and often do finish first.

Nice is a four-letter word whose application is never off color. N should never be for nasty or negative.

O is for obligation.

Your first obligation to your company and employees is to set them up for success.

P is for pride.

Take pride in your company. Take pride in your employees. Take pride in your products. But check your personal pride at the door. Pride is the stone over which many people stumble.

Q is for qualifications.

Help your employees develop the qualifications they need to take the next step in their careers.

R is for right.

Always make time to do it right the first time. Otherwise you'll have to take time to do it over.

S is for sales.

A manager needs to sell ideas, plans and products to staff before a project can take off. Five-word job description of a CEO: Best salesperson in the place.

T is for team.

The people who make it big in business are those who are able to put together a team and know what to do with it. Support your team, department, and organization. For all-star results, be a team player.

U is for up front.

Being up front builds trust. Customers and employees appreciate honesty and will be more willing to work with people who respect them enough to tell them when there's a problem.

V is for versatile.

Of the many skills managers need to bring to the job, versatility is key to understanding and relating to different challenges they face daily.

W is for walk your plant or office floor at least once a day.

Be visible and available. It will keep you firmly grounded in the knowledge of what business you're really in.

X is for eXpert.

Spend at least 10 percent of your budget on the best professional advice available before you spend a nickel on anything else. If you can't be an expert, hire an expert.

Y is for yesterday.

The decisions you made yesterday will determine where you go tomorrow.

Z is for zenith.

An exceptional manager guides a company to its zenith.

Mackay's Moral:
Managing people is an art;
strive for a masterpiece.

THE ABCs of
TEAM-BUILDING

I had the pleasure of joining a panel that addressed specific challenges of changing business practices in the 21st century. We heard so many questions about how organizations can function best in an era of flexible hours, working remotely, and limited face-to-face interactions.

It inspired me to develop the ABCs of team-building, a topic that seems particularly popular in this era of reorganizations, layoffs, and downsizing. The following concepts are what I consider the fundamentals of team-building.

A is for action.

No team can function without a plan of action, even when the final outcome is to take no action at all. Actions speak louder than words.

B is for brainpower.

If two heads are better than one, I would submit that a cohesive, well-assembled team should have enough brainpower to attack any project.

C is for cooperation and communication.

Team members need to cooperate, even if they don't necessarily agree. Clear communication is the roadmap to cooperation. Communication requires both effective sending and receiving.

D is for dedication.

As members of a team, you must be dedicated to the goals of the team, or you are on the wrong team. There are no shortcuts in life.

E is for ears.

Use your ears more than your mouth because listening skills are critical for team success. If you want to be heard, you must know how to listen.

F is for fun.

Work should be fun, and working together is usually a lot more fun than working alone. Fun and work should go hand in hand.

G is for the group effort.

The motto needs to be "all for one and one for all" in order to be a real team. Michael Jordan said, "There is no 'I' in team, but there is in win."

H is for help.

We all need help at some time. Don't be afraid to ask for it. The fool asks the wise for advice, but the wise ask the experienced.

I is for the ideas

that come from brainstorming and picking each others' brains. Let the ideas flow and then choose those which hold the most potential.

J is for juggling.

Combining all the company's needs and desired results will often require a juggling act, but a competent team will be able to achieve that balance.

K is for kinetic–

energetic, dynamic team members keep things moving.

Successful people generally have lots of energy. And many people believe the better your energy, the more likely you'll get what you want.

L is for leadership.

Every team needs a leader, and every leader needs to be able to depend on the team. Good leaders bring out the best in employees. Good leaders develop more than good employees, they develop more good leaders.

M is for motivation.

Nothing motivates a team like trust placed in them by management to solve a problem. Motivation is the spark that ignites success.

N is for negotiate.

Give and take is as important within a team as it is with outside clients. You can't negotiate anything unless you absolutely know the market. Only then you will be able to recognize a good deal when you see it.

O is for objective.

Team members need to understand the intended objective of the project, and be willing to expand their perspectives to find the best answers.

P is for planning.

A plan doesn't need to be rigid to be effective, but it must provide enough direction to keep the team on course.

Q is for quirks.

Accept that team members will have some quirks. Use them to your advantage.

R is for resolution.

The whole point of forming a team is to work together to achieve results. Resolving differences of opinions may lead to results that may not be what had been originally anticipated.

S is for solutions,

which differ from results in that there may be more than one solution to any given problem. Then the team can implement the best choice.

T is for time management.

A well-managed team uses their meeting and planning time efficiently, and understands when it is time to finish the project. Killing time isn't murder; it's suicide.

U is for unity.

Once a decision is made, the team needs to be unified to implement the plans. If the team can't act as a unit, then it may be necessary to reconfigure the team.

V is for validation.

Every team member has to have a voice in the proceedings, and it is up to the team leader to insure that all members feel their opinions are validated.

W is for work ethic.

Each member needs to complete the given assignments and should have confidence that others will demonstrate the same commitment.

X is the X factor

– the chemistry that makes a team productive because all members are committed to the same goal.

Y is for yes – say it as often as you can.

"Yes, I can help. Yes, that's a good idea. Yes, let's move ahead. Yes, we did it!"

Z is for Zoom

– a tremendous tool for times your team can't meet in person.

Mackay's Moral:
The team you build will determine
the business you build.

THE ABCs of
RISK-TAKING

One of the reasons we admire people who take risks is that most of us are scared stiff at the prospect of taking risks ourselves. "I could never do something like that," we say. The "something" we could never do might be anything from starting a new career to learning how to cook something. It doesn't matter. Sometimes it seems that the only people who can take risks successfully are the people who have nothing to lose.

Fortunately, most of us will never have to worry about taking monumental risks. Of course, we use that to downplay the importance of the risks we *do* face. If it's not something that involves real, measurable danger – skydiving, for example – it's clearly not important as far as risks go. What you really mean is that you think the fear you feel about your "small" risk is misplaced – an overreaction.

In short, playing it safe isn't the way to get ahead. You've got to go out on a limb sometimes – but not so far that you fall off. To help you, I've come up with my ABCs of risk-taking.

A is for apprehension.

Taking a large or small risk comes with a degree of apprehension. I consider that a healthy reaction; you should have to invest some serious consideration into making a bold move.

B is for bravery.

Afraid to try something new? Most people are. But it's all over so soon that regrets will invariably be for what you didn't do rather than for what you did. The secret ingredient is bravery.

C is for challenging.

Don't be afraid to take calculated risks. If you win, you will be happy. If you lose, you will be wise.

D is for differentiator.

Some risks can make or break your business. Differentiators understand that progress depends on finding new and better ways to accomplish goals, thereby improving their chances of success.

E is for enterprising.

Thinking outside the box to find the information you need or to get the project accomplished is one of the traits that I really admire in people. Resourcefulness is a real asset for anyone trying to get the edge over the competition. It's also an essential element of risk.

F is for flexibility.

Nearly all the successful people I know have dealt with defeat, slumps, failures, change and adversities of every nature. The reason they are successful despite all that is they had the confidence and courage to face those setbacks and find a way to overcome them. For some, it was pure stubbornness; for others, it was refusal to admit defeat.

G is for genius.

Recognizing a genius idea is one of the traits that characterizes serious risk-takers. They can spot potential in tiny changes or see the need for complete overhauls. Then they find a way to do it.

H is for healthy.

Approach risk with a healthy skepticism, then assess the real hazards and benefits to reach a reasonable path to fulfillment.

I is for inherent.

From taking your first step to investing your life savings in a new venture, nearly every activity we undertake in our lives involves taking risks. Once you understand the hidden dangers or obstacles, you can manage risk much easier.

J is for jealousy.

Never take a risk out of jealousy for another's accomplishments, because it will end in disaster. Instead, study their success and learn how they turned risk into success.

K is for knock it out of the park.

You can't hit a homerun unless you take a swing at the ball. Keep your eye on the ball, and when you see an opportunity, crush it.

L is for leap of faith.

Every major decision, from marriages to mergers – regardless of the supporting advice, statistics, reports, and studies – requires a leap of faith. In the final analysis, what your inner voice tells you is the best advice you can get.

M is for mission.

A clearly defined mission makes managing risk considerably easier. If you know where you want to go, you can anticipate some of the landmines along the way.

N is for nerve.

Risk-taking often requires nerves of steel to face the inevitable challenges and failures involved with big risks. Being able to keep your nerves steady prevents you from giving up when the going gets tough.

O is for originality.

Hanging around with creative people helps you understand different ways of looking at the world and stimulates your thought processes to more original ideas. That's an essential element of risk-taking, allowing you to develop your projects from a new perspective.

P is for possibilities.

When you see what is possible, you are more inclined to take a risk that will pay off.

Q is for quit.

Quit complaining, quit dragging your feet, quit talking yourself out of what could be a fabulous opportunity because you are afraid to take the risk. Quit being afraid of succeeding.

R is for realistic.

Taking risks can reap big rewards, but only if the venture is realistic. Pie-in-the-sky ideas are not actually risks, they are folly. If you have a plan and can honestly see a path to success, that's a realistic risk.

S is for stepping out of your comfort zone.

No risk, no success. Know risk, know success.

T is for turtles.

A turtle only makes progress when it sticks its neck out. Taking a risk means sticking your neck out instead of hiding in your shell and staying in the same place.

U is for undaunted.

Understand that failure will happen. There will be some pain and failure. It's part of life. You need to fully understand what you are risking.

V is for visionaries,

the risk-takers who don't see things as they are, rather as they could be. Visionaries exercise a lot more control over the outcome of events. You don't achieve your dreams by playing it safe.

W is for willpower,

which keeps people hammering away. Determined people possess the stamina and courage to pursue their ambitions despite criticism, ridicule or unfavorable circumstances. In fact, discouragement usually spurs them on to greater things. When they get discouraged, they recognize that in order to change their results, some change is in order.

X is for eXhilarating.

Young people especially take risks for the thrill and as part of normal development. Risk-taking can build confidence and strengthen decision-making skills.

Y is for yes you can.

When others say no you can't, and you see a better way forward, ignore the nay-sayers and tell yourself yes you can. Then accept the risk and show them how it's done.

Z is for zinger.

When you get a zinger of an idea, zero in on how you can make it happen. There's no greater feeling in business than to know the risks you take are paying off.

Mackay's Moral:
Sometimes it's risky
not to take a risk.

THE ABCs of LEADERSHIP

As children, we played "follow the leader" for hours on end. The crazier the route and antics, the more we liked it. Being the leader was the best part.

As working adults, "follow the leader" takes on a whole new meaning. Leadership is an art and a skill. It's hard work that is extremely rewarding and occasionally completely thankless. What traits make a great leader? These are my thoughts.

A is for accountability.

When President Harry Truman said "The buck stops here," he was demonstrating that he was willing to take the blame along with the praise. Leaders accept responsibility for their actions as well as those that report to them. I want to own my decisions. I am willing to accept the blame when necessary as well as the credit when deserved for my actions.

B is for boundaries.

Effective leaders respect personal and professional boundaries. In other words, they never expect their followers to do something they would not do themselves.

C is for courage.

Tough times and tough choices require courageous leaders. Doing the right thing instead of the easy thing is a mark of courage. It's advantageous to be courageous.

D is for decisions.

Good decision-making skills are priceless. Remember, not making a decision is a decision in itself.

E is for excitement.

A leader must be excited about their job, their goals, their staff, and their potential. They need to exemplify a TGIM attitude – Thank God It's Monday.

F is for fearless.

Leaders should adopt Franklin Roosevelt's philosophy: "The only thing we have to fear is fear itself." Leaders must not be afraid to be bold.

G is for growth.

This includes your growth as a leader, your employees' growth to reach their potential and your company's growth to achieve goals.

H is for heart.

A good decision must factor in the human element. When your head and your heart say the same thing, you can bet it's the right answer.

I is for influence.

Leadership doesn't mean getting people to just do their jobs; it means getting people to do their best.

J is for judgment.

A leader must demonstrate consistently good judgment in order to set the standard for the organization. Followers depend on consistent, level-headed judgment.

K is for knowledge.

No one expects leaders to know everything, but everyone expects leaders to know whom to ask when they don't have the information at hand.

L is for legendary.

We can all name people who make it look easy to run a company or volunteer organization. Legendary leaders are the role models who people want to work for, learn from, and be compared to.

M is for magnanimous.

Leaders must rise above pettiness and meanness.

N is for new.

Never be afraid to try something new, even if the old way isn't broken. The results might be better than you expected.

O is for organization.

This is a two-fer: your personal organization and the organization you lead. Your office may be a disaster area, but make sure your mind is organized. The organization you lead should always be foremost on your list of priorities.

P is for professionalism.

You need to set a clear example to the people you lead, and make sure they know what you expect from them.

Q is for quick-thinking.

A leader must be able to think on the spot, even if the answer is "we need to give this more thought." A leader can figure out the difference.

R is for recognition.

Be sure to heap recognition on those who have worked hard and achieved. Sharing the credit doesn't diminish you, it demonstrates your ability to hire well and acknowledge achievement.

S is for strength.

A strong leader never wavers on values, ethics or commitment. That's a very tall order, but absolutely essential.

T is for team-builder.

Whether you are a team of two or two thousand, as a leader you are also cheerleader-in-chief. "Go, team, go" only works if you provide the right environment.

U is for ubiquitous.

Your presence and influence must be felt everywhere. Make sure the team knows whom to follow.

V is for visible.

Not only should your presence be felt, you should be personally present at events large and small. Get to know your staff beyond their working titles.

W is for wisdom.

No one is born wise, but some people learn faster than others what makes an organization tick.

X is for eXample.

If you want people to follow the leader, you must set a proper course. Inspire those you lead with your example.

Y is for yeoman's service.

A leader has to be willing to work harder than everyone else in the organization. Adopt a servant mentality to be a truly effective leader.

Z is for zest.

Let your passion show, and see if it isn't contagious!

Mackay's Moral:

Take the lead and be a superstar!

THE ABCs of
CREATIVITY

Creativity fuels innovation, and innovation is essential to business. So I'm sharing my thoughts on creativity, yet I'm using one of my favorite formulas: a simple list of ABCs.

While the ABC approach itself may not be entirely creative, I think the message will bear me out. I have covered the topics that I believe are the most important concepts in business over the years. But unless you use them creatively, they are just words. Put these lists to work for you.

Now it's time to dissect creativity. Truly successful people understand the fundamental value of setting yourself apart from the competition, or finding a creative way to stand out from the crowd.

A is for advertising.

Expand your brand beyond media-generated advertising. For example, we painted our company name and phone numbers on top of our delivery trucks so it was visible to people who worked on upper floors of tall buildings.

B is for bold.

People are not inspired by ordinary messages, so give them a reason to remember you. Be bold. Do what the ordinary fear.

C is for curious.

Curiosity may not have been good for the cat, but it's a winning formula for people. Be curious about everything around you. To the great thinkers, curiosity is essential. We all need to question what we do not understand, and keep asking until we find answers. Will we solve all the mysteries of the universe? Probably not, but we didn't get to the moon by wishing on a star.

D is for different.

Don't be afraid to do things that have never been tried before. You have to have enough faith in yourself to trust your instincts. When was the last time you tried something new?

E is for everyone.

I firmly believe everyone has the capacity to be creative, if only they allow themselves to be. There is no correlation between IQ and creativity. Every single person can become way more creative than they ever imagined.

F is for funny.

Most products or services can benefit from a creative and humorous approach. When you make people laugh, or make them feel good, they are more likely to remember.

G is for genuine.

Creativity does not include stretching the truth. Be genuine, be real, be authentic.

H is for head.

Use yours to go to the head of the creativity class. Think big, think bold, think creative, think stretch, think quantum leaps. Think vision, think speed, think customize, think focus, think flexible.

I is for ideas,

which are like rabbits.

If you can get a couple, pretty soon you have a dozen. However, ideas without action are worthless.

J is for January, which is International Creativity Month

– a time to remind individuals and organizations around the globe to capitalize on the power of creativity. Creativity is important all year long.

K is for kids.

Kids are unafraid to take gigantic risks. They haven't been trained yet to take the safe approach. Creativity comes naturally to kids. Pay attention to your inner child.

L is for light bulb,

like the ones in the comic strips.

When you get a sudden spark of brilliance, make note of it immediately. Do you know how many products, services, ad campaigns, even Broadway plays started out as a scribble on a cocktail napkin? However you record it, just don't lose that thought.

M is for mistakes.

Give yourself permission to try things even if you're not sure they'll succeed. Often you'll stumble across a different strategy or a better path along the way.

N is for nature.

New evidence suggests you can boost your imagination and creativity by getting outside and spending some time in nature. Take a walk and clear out the cobwebs.

O is for omnivorous –

take in everything.

Let ideas develop before you dismiss them. Creativity has no script; it is inspired ad libbing. Be aware of what is going on around you.

P is for patience.

You can't hurry creativity, so take time to ponder your ideas. Sit back and think things over. Let the seeds of ideas bloom into full flower. Patience takes practice.

Q is for quest.

When you are on a quest for new business or promoting a new product or service, you need to employ every creative strategy that you can muster.

R is for relax.

Most people are at their creative best when they are relaxed and not under pressure. Give your subconscious a chance to work by turning your brain off from time to time. Take time to exercise and relax, and give yourself permission to think about other things. A tired mind won't generate fresh ideas.

S is for simple.

No, this is not a contradiction. Creativity need not be complicated to be effective. Sometimes a simple approach is the most creative. It only takes a little spark to ignite a great fire.

T is for thinking outside the box.

Look for a fresh perspective or unconventional method instead of the same tired approach. Boxes are great for storing things. Just don't store your brain there.

U is for understanding your limitations,

and then finding a creative way to blast beyond them.

To get what you've never had, you must do what you've never done.

V is for variety.

Variety truly is the spice of life. Changes and new experiences make life more interesting.

W is for wonder.

Creativity embraces the wonder of novelty and ingenuity, and turns them into wonderful results.

X is for eXceed expectations.

(That is my creative spelling.) Find creative ways to achieve awesome outcomes.

Y is for yesterday.

If you did it yesterday, it's not creative today. Look toward tomorrow instead.

Z is for zeitgeist.

Catch the spirit of creativity!

Mackay's Moral:
*Start every day with a healthy dose
of vitamin C — Creativity!*

THE ABCs of
PUBLIC SPEAKING

It's been said there are two times in life when you are truly alone: just before you die and just before you deliver a five-minute speech. Stage fright can be terrifying, but it needn't be paralyzing.

Delivering over a thousand speeches teaches a person a thing or two about getting through to the audience. Because I am often asked for advice from nervous speakers, I have developed my ABCs of public speaking.

A is for audience.

Learn all you can about those who will be in attendance so that you can tailor your remarks to hold their interest. Always try and find one or two people in the audience who you know or deserve recognition before you give your speech and acknowledge them. WOW! They will be surprised and love it.

B is for body language.

Move around, gesture, and use facial expressions to demonstrate your enthusiasm for your topic. Actions sometimes speak louder than words. If you want to get a leg up, learn how to use effective body language.

C is for creativity.

Don't be afraid to use props, PowerPoint or audience participation to add sparkle and surprise. Even the most serious topics can benefit from a creative approach to make them memorable.

D is for deliver.

Your presentation needs to have a focused message that leaves the audience with significant take-home value.

E is for eye contact,

a critical feature of an effective speaker.

Connecting with your audience can't happen without it. When you fail to make eye contact with your listeners, you look less authoritative, less believable.

F is for feedback.

Ask for immediate, unfiltered responses so you can continue to improve your skills. And don't forget to debrief yourself after the event, including what worked well and what didn't.

G is for grammar.

Pay attention to the language you use. Make certain it is correct and concise.

H is for homework.

Study the organization you are addressing: What are the problems, issues, concerns, and opportunties? Mispronouncing names is unforgivable.

I is for introduction.

Make sure that the person introducing you is a real pro, not someone who is a poor speaker being given the honor because of their status in an organization. Provide a prepared introduction with your pertinent information.

J is for jokes.

Try them out on several people to make sure they are appropriate and amusing. Plays don't open up on Broadway, they open in New Haven. Humor, anecdotes, and stories add so much to a speech as long as they are not offensive.

K is for know your audience.

Speakers have to demonstrate a real grasp of the subject at hand in order to be taken seriously.

L is for lighting.

Studies show that people laugh more and retain more in brightly lit rooms. Dim the lights only if you are using PowerPoint presentations, and only as long as necessary.

M is for masking tape.

Seal noisy door latches to avoid distractions. Block off the back rows of chairs to keep the audience up front.

N is for noise,

which is a real attention killer.

After-dinner speakers especially have to compete with clearing tables and clinking glasses. Consult with the host organization about minimizing noise interruptions.

O is for opening.

In order to grab the audience's attention immediately, you need a spectacular opener. Don't give a speech until you have one.

P is for practice, practice, practice.

Know your stuff inside and out. There is no substitute for preparation.

Q is for Q&A.

Start the Q&A five minutes before you are ready to close, so that you have the last word and control the ending. Since most people are shy about asking the first question, break the awkward silence by announcing this and saying, "Can I have the second question?"

R is for room size.

If you have any control over the venue, insist that the room seat only the planned number of audience members. A room that is too big destroys rapport. You want the excitement of a standing room only, bumper-to-bumper crowd. Encourage people to sit down front. If there is extra space at the back of the room, put up screens or dividers to cut down the excess space. Also, try to avoid high-ceiling rooms.

S is for style.

Develop your own signature style. Study the great speakers and identify what makes them unique. Then call on your strengths to bolster your message. Let the audience see that you are pleased/happy/honored to be asked to speak.

T is for Toastmasters International,

the organization that I recommend for anyone who wants to hone their speaking skills. It's tremendous training for speakers at all levels of ability. Check out the Toastmaster chapter in your area.

U is for unforgettable.

Make your speech memorable with a well-organized message peppered with clever stories and examples sprinkled with humor and wrapped up with a great summary.

V is for voice.

Listen to yourself on tape so that you can adjust tempo, tone, timing, and inflection.

W is for wit.

You want your message to teach and inform. I'm particularly fond of starting the lessons in my speeches with a "Mackay's Moral," witty words of wisdom that drive home my point.

X is for eXperience.

The best way to become a better speaker is to speak as often as you can. There is no substitute for experience.

Y is for you.

Take pains to look your best. First impressions count. Don't let the message be overshadowed by a careless messenger.

Z is for zip it up.

A smashing closing is as important as a gripping opening.

Here is one more way to give an A-plus presentation: Check out my speaking tips handout, "Harvey Mackay's 35 To Stay Alive," available for free on my website, www.harveymackayacademy.com under Resources.

Mackay's Moral:
*The best way to sound like you
know what you're talking about is
to know what you're talking about.*

THE ABCs for REACHING YOUR DREAMS

I often joke that it takes years to become an overnight success. But it starts with a dream. My dream was to own a factory. I wasn't even sure what kind of product I'd make, or exactly where it would be. But I pictured myself walking the factory floor, talking to workers. The pile of broken-down machines I bought might have looked more like a nightmare at the time. But dreams come true – with a lot of wide-awake work.

Here are my ABCs for reaching your dreams.

A is for attitude.

It is absolutely essential that you have a positive mental attitude in every aspect of life. Stay upbeat no matter what happens. Your attitude determines your altitude.

B is for believe in yourself, even when no one else does.

Don't ever let anyone tell you that you can't accomplish your goals. It doesn't matter if *they* say you can't do it. The only thing that matters is if *you* say it.

C is for change it up.

Your dream might not even be original. You can start with an existing idea, product or service, and then use your innovative skills to take it to a new level.

D is for determination,

what keeps us hammering away.

Determined people possess the stamina and courage to pursue their ambitions despite criticism, ridicule, or unfavorable circumstances.

E is for enthusiasm.

You should be so pumped about your dream that you won't take no for an answer. Get excited about what you can accomplish. Enthusiasm is the spark that ignites our lives.

F is for focus.

Don't let distractions and interruptions undermine your focus. Keep your eye on the prize. Stay focused as best you can, and don't let things happen to you – not when you can make things happen. The person who is everywhere is nowhere.

G is for get started.

Get up and get going or your dreams will never be more than a charming idea. Better to chase a dream than to be pursued by regrets.

H is for hard work.

Be prepared to work long and hard to make your dreams come true. You might lose some sleep achieving your dreams, but rest assured, it will be worth it. Hard work and perseverance will keep your dreams from becoming just wishful thinking.

I is for imagination.

As you explore possibilities, give your mind some space to wander to new territory. Anyone who thinks the sky is the limit has limited imagination.

J is for just do it!

Ideas don't work unless you do. People begin to become successful the minute they decide to be.

K is for keep dreaming.

Often times one idea will lead to another and then another. Watch your dreams grow. Dreamers have a way of scoring big triumphs.

L is for learn everything that is important to you.

Take classes, find mentors, search online – there's a world of information available just waiting for you.

M is for magnify.

Put your dreams under a magnifying glass to see where you can improve your ideas and watch them grow.

N is for no.

Know when to say, "No, we need to try a new approach."

O is for open mind.

Consider options that could improve your ideas and make adjustments as needed. If you can imagine it, you can achieve it. If you can dream it, you can become it.

P is for perfection.

In your dreams, your concept is perfect. Work out the kinks, shake out the wrinkles, and keep trying until you can't do any better.

Q is for quagmire.

You need to be prepared to face difficult challenges along the way – just don't get stuck in the mud.

R is for results.

As I often say, they don't pay off on effort, they pay off on results. Your dream may take some time to achieve, but until you produce results, it's still just a dream.

S is for strategy.

A strategy connects where you are and where you want to go. Do something every day that puts you a step closer to achieving the dream.

T is for tenacity.

Take control of your own destiny. It helps to have a little bulldog in you to achieve your dreams.

U is for unique.

Lots of people may have the same dream as you, but you are unique in your ability, desire, and knowledge.

V is for visualize your dreams.

I believe that visualization is one of the most powerful means of achieving personal goals. If seeing is believing, visualizing is achieving.

W is for what's next.

When you have realized your dream, start dreaming again. You'll be amazed how much easier it becomes to dream even bigger dreams once you try.

X is for eXperiment.

Use your experience to experiment with different ideas and solutions.

Y is for YOUR dreams.

Make sure you are not chasing someone else's dreams. Your dreams should have your fingerprints all over them.

Z is for ZZZs

– a great place to start dreaming.

Mackay's Moral:
May all your dreams come true.

THE ABCs of
SUCCESS

Success is a journey, not a destination. You may take a few detours, hit some roadblocks and arrive at a different place than you planned.

Success comes in many forms and means different things to different people. In the working world, it is often defined as landing the perfect job, achieving a targeted income level, occupying a corner office or owning a business. However you measure it, success is sweet. And it doesn't happen overnight.

Here are my ABCs of success to help you be successful.

A is for adversity.

I have never met a successful person who hasn't had to overcome either a little or a lot of adversity.

B is for boredom.

Never let yourself get bored. It's the kiss of death for anyone who wants to get ahead in life, and even worse for anyone who truly wants to love what they do.

C is for competition.

The existence of competition is a good sign. Nobody ever set a world's record competing against himself. Let your competition push you to succeed.

D is for demonstrate.

Find concrete ways to demonstrate how valuable your presence is to the company, your customers, and your community.

E is for eagerness.

The successful people I know display an eagerness to improve and get the job done. They have a carrot in front of them, slightly out of reach, no matter how many carrots they already have.

F is for faults.

Few of us lead unblemished personal or professional lives. It's the ability to overcome and learn from our faults, rather than never to experience them, that counts.

G is for guarantees.

There are none in this life, but there are creative ways to better your chances. You can, however, guarantee your customers and co-workers that they can depend on you to always give your best.

H is for happiness.

To me, happiness is the key to success, not vice versa. Only you can draw the map of the road to your happiness.

I is for I'll take care of it.

There will always be a place for the person who says "I'll take care of it." And then does it.

J is for job.

There is something unique and memorable about each one of us. It's our job to find out what it is and let other people in on the secret.

K is for keen.

You must develop a keen sense of what your customer wants, what your company needs from you, and the best way to deliver both.

L is for love what you do, do what you love,

and you'll never have to work another day in your life. That's my idea of success.

M is for morals.

A solid moral compass is critical to succeeding. Anything less than stellar ethics diminishes success.

N is for navigating shark-infested waters,

and learning how to swim with the sharks.

O is for optimism.

Optimists are people who make the best of it when they get the worst of it.

P is for persistence.

Much of what makes people successful is persistence. Instead of giving myself reasons why I can't, I give myself reasons why I can. Persistence is one of the traits I look for in hiring any new employee, especially a sales rep. There is no substitute.

Q is for quintessential.

Successful people always strive to be the quintessential example of quality and decency.

R is for resourceful,

because resourceful people can see the upside of down times.

They are not willing to give up just because things get complicated. They don't accept defeat easily.

S is for success.

If you want to double your success ratio, you might have to double your failure rate.

T is for things others don't like to do.

We all have to do things that we don't particularly enjoy, but successful people do them so they can do the things they enjoy.

U is for university.

Most people drive an average of 12,000 miles a year. If you live to be 75, that's 3 ½ years in a car. Turn your car into a university and listen to self-help podcasts and motivational lessons.

V is for victory.

Celebrate victories, large and small, along the road to success and be sure to thank those who helped you along the way.

W is for work.

It's not enough to work hard or work smart. You have to work hard and smart. Work isn't work if you like it. There are many formulas for success, but none of them works unless you do.

X is for eXchange of ideas.

Unless you are able to communicate, to master the basic skills of speaking and writing in a forceful, polite, effective way, the day is going to come when what you've learned won't be enough. Entertain a variety of ideas to achieve the best results.

Y is for Yoda.

Yes, the Jedi master. Everyone benefits from mentors like Yoda in their quests to succeed. Once you have achieved success, pass along the tradition and be a Yoda for those who can benefit from your guidance.

Z is for zone.

When you are in the zone, things just click. Success is all but guaranteed. When you find your zone, let it take you to the top of your game.

Mackay's Moral:
Some people succeed because
they are destined to,
but most people succeed because
they are determined to.

Acknowledgments

First, and I do mean first, my profound thanks to my Chief of Staff Greg Bailey who has been with me for more than 25 years and has made pivotal contributions to this book. Greg continues to be my right hand – and so much more. Greg has an effortless ease in sourcing topics and keeping projects on schedule, all with a fanatical attention to detail.

Mary Anne Bailey has been part of my "kitchen cabinet" since the 1990s. Her help in researching, organizing, fact checking, and proofreading is insurmountable. She has a mastery in polishing prose and is a consummate professional with unlimited knowledge and patience.

My sister Margie Resnick Blickman has an eagle's eye for detail and remains as astute and valuable as ever. She has been a tremendous sounding board over my entire career.

Neil Naftalin is another member of my "kitchen cabinet." I run everything I write by him because of his meticulous fact-checking.

Thanks to Bryan Heathman and all the people at Made for Success Publishing, including DeeDee Heathman, Tyler Heathman, and Katie Rios.

My cover photographer, Stephanie Rau, brought the best out of me and managed to find my "good side."

Valerie Boyd of Valerie Boyd Design has helped design several of my book covers, including this one, and was also instrumental in the internal design.

Our Executive Assistant, Karen Thompson, is the unrivaled utility player on our team. We value her agility and skill in shifting gears to the varied needs of an often hectic office.

My business partner, Scott Mitchell, CEO of MackayMitchell Envelope Company, and all of our hard-working employees who practice the principles in this book, keep me on my toes in this ever-changing business world.

And to my family, my wife of more than 60 years, Carol Ann, and our 3 wonderful children, David, Mimi, and Jojo, and their families keep me forever grateful. They may be last here, but they are first in my heart always.

About the Author

Harvey Mackay has written seven *New York Times* bestselling books, three reached #1, and two were named by the *Times* among the top 15 inspirational business books of all time: *Swim With the Sharks Without Being Eaten Alive* and *Beware the Naked Man Who Offers You His Shirt.*

Harvey's latest book, *You Haven't Hit Your Peak Yet!*, debuted on Jan. 29, 2020. His other books include *The Mackay MBA of Selling in the Real World* (November 2011), *Use Your Head to Get Your Foot in the Door: Job Search Secrets No One Else Will Tell You* (2010), *We Got Fired! … And It's the Best Thing That*

Ever Happened To Us (2004), *Pushing the Envelope* (1999), and *Dig Your Well Before You're Thirsty: The Only Networking Book You'll Ever Need* (1997). His books have sold 10 million copies in 80 countries and have been translated in 52 languages.

For the last 29 years, Harvey has been a nationally syndicated columnist. His weekly articles appear in 100 newspapers and magazines around the country, including the *Minneapolis Star Tribune and the Arizona Republic*.

He is one of America's most popular and entertaining business speakers for Fortune 500-size companies and associations, and has spoken on six continents. Toastmasters International named him one of the top five speakers in the world, and he is a member of the National Speakers Association Hall of Fame.

In addition, Harvey is chairman of MackayMitchell Envelope Company, a $100 million company he founded at age 26. MackayMitchell has 400 employees and manufactures 25 million envelopes a day.

Harvey is a graduate of the University of Minnesota and the Stanford University Graduate School of Business Executive Program. He is an avid runner and marathoner, having run 10 marathons, and is a former #1 ranked senior tennis player in Minnesota.

The American Management Association listed Harvey among the top 30 leaders who influenced business in 2014, which also included Colin Powell, Jack Welch, and Richard Branson. In July 2015, Forbes said, "Harvey Mackay is one of the world's top leadership experts who has accomplished more in business than most entrepreneurs could achieve in their lifetimes."

In April 2004, Harvey received the prestigious Horatio Alger Award in the Supreme Court Chambers. Previous recipients include Presidents Eisenhower, Ford, and Reagan, former Secretary of State Colin Powell and entertainer Oprah Winfrey.

He was inducted into the Minnesota Business Hall of Fame in 2002. He is the past president of the Minneapolis Chamber of Commerce, the Envelope Manufacturers Association of America, the University of Minnesota National Alumni Association, to name only a few. In October 2008, he was presented the University of Minnesota Outstanding Achievement Award, the highest award presented to an alumnus.

He played a key role in bringing the 1992 Super Bowl to Minneapolis, along with serving as the catalyst in bringing an NBA franchise (Minnesota Timberwolves) to his home state, serving as chairman of the task force in getting the Hubert H. Humphrey Metrodome built, recruiting Lou Holtz to coach the University of Minnesota football team, and many more.

All of which is why *Fortune* magazine refers to him as "Mr. Make Things Happen."

Closing Thoughts

If you have thoughts, comments, or ideas about this book, I'd love to hear from you. (Please, no requests for personal advice.)

Write to me at the following address:

Harvey Mackay
MackayMitchell Envelope Company 2100 Elm St. SE
Minneapolis, MN 55414

You can reach me at my email, harvey@mackay.com or my website, www.harveymackay.com.